TWICE ENSLAVED

LIBERTY AND JUSTICE FOR HENRIETTA WOOD

TWICE ENSLAVED

LIBERTY AND JUSTICE FOR HENRIETTA WOOD

SELENE CASTROVILLA   ILLUSTRATED BY ERIN K. ROBINSON

CALKINS CREEK
AN IMPRINT OF ASTRA BOOKS FOR YOUNG READERS
New York

To Orel Protopopescu — *SC*

For my cousin Sydney.

Thank you for your brilliant, inspiring words …

I can't help but think Henrietta connected us. — *EKR*

Contents

PART ONE
COMING OF AGE

Growing Pains

Henrietta Wood was born in 1820
on the wrong side
of the Ohio River.
From the time she could stand,
she watched
the river's current pulsing
over the long mile
between Kentucky's slavery
and Indiana's freedom.
From the time she could walk,
she watched
a ferry crossing
between the two states.
From the time she could scrub,
Moses Tousey, her enslaver,
who owned that ferry too,
made her work on his farm.
From the time she knew what freedom meant,
he watched her, making sure
that there would be no ride across the river for her,
no ride to liberty.

Uprooting

Fourteen-year-old Henrietta,
in rattling shackles,
was taken away
from the farm,
taken away
from her parents,
taken away
from her little brother Joshua
with the scar on his chin
from a hot coffeepot.
Down a rutted road
on a bone-rattling cart,
she was taken away
with her other brothers and sister,
huddled together
on a hundred-mile ride
alongside the Ohio River,
along the line between free and slave,
taken down to Louisville, Kentucky,
a city nothing like the farm
on the Ohio River's edge.
Nothing was the same,
nothing but the river
that held her prisoner
on its wrong side.

Selection

Pushed into a pen,
pushed and locked in with others,
so many others, enslaved like her,
Henrietta heard the chilling news:
they would be sold
to the highest bidder,
delivered like goods
into the hands of strangers.
She prayed not to be alone,
prayed to hold on to
her brothers and sister.
But the next day
she was sold
without them.
Henrietta craned her neck
for one last look
before she was alone,
without family,
sold to a mean man,
a rich man
named Henry Forsyth,
who did not care
about her one bit.

Hardships

For two years, she was forced
to do cooking, washing, and scrubbing,
forced to do the hard work
of keeping Forsyth's home,
forced to endure his raging temper
and the vicious floggings
he inflicted with his whip.
There was no pleasing him,
no moving him,
although she cried in pain,
cried in sorrow.
But losing her family,
that loneliness hurt far more
than the most brutal lashing.

Down to Hell

When Forsyth lost his fortune,
Henrietta finally rode
the majestic Ohio River,
but not across
to Indiana,
not to freedom.
Sold again,
to William Cirode,
she was carried south,
down where the river
entered a longer river,
the Mississippi.
Carried on a massive steamboat,
smoke clouding the sky,
whistle shrilling,
burnt wood tainting the air.
Each turn
of the boat's paddle wheel
delivered her
down to where there was no freedom
on either side of the river,
down seven hundred miles
to Louisiana, New Orleans,
a city enslaved people called "Hell."
If you were brought there,
to the sweltering heat,
where slavery was so harsh,
so cruel,
it was near impossible
to ever leave.

Prayers

Trapped in the humid heat,
working up a sweat,
working in Cirode's household,
cooking, cleaning, ironing,
working hard to please his family,
Henrietta tried not to think
about her family
hundreds of miles away.
But sometimes late at night,
curled up alone in the dark,
she could not think
of anything but those
she had lost.
Dear Lord,
she prayed,
please deliver me from
this hell.
He had never answered
her prayers
but she kept trying.
The Lord was all
she had.

PART TWO

A SWEET TASTE OF LIBERTY

Restoration

Henrietta toiled
in that burning hell
for several years,
left her teenage self
and entered adulthood,
when her prayer
was answered.
Cirode left his wife, Jane,
and she took possession
of Henrietta.
Jane brought Henrietta
back from hell,
up the pulsing rivers,
first the Mississippi,
and then the Ohio.
All the way to Louisville,
a different hell,
to glimpsing freedom
just a mile away.
Back where she had been torn
from her brothers and sister.
Where were they now?
And her parents
and little Joshua?
Her wounded heart
ached just as much
as that day she'd been auctioned.
Why had one prayer been granted,
but others ignored?

Happiness

Jane left Henrietta in Louisville,
hiring her out to work for others,
where soon she discovered a person
among the enslaved
who looked like Joshua.
Could this man be that boy?
Smoothing her fingers over
his whiskered chin,
she found the coffee-scalded scar,
the prettiest spot on his face,
and her fingers read *joy*!
Henrietta threw her arms
around his neck,
telling the shocked fellow
he was her brother.
He rejoiced with her,
exchanging
hug for hug.
Sister and brother
talked about
the ten years
they'd been parted.
Ten years of not knowing
what had happened
to the rest of their family,
a hidden scar
they shared.
Henrietta felt sure
they would all
reunite in heaven
and they would have
quite a talk,
long as the river.
For now, being with Joshua
was heaven on earth.

The Miracle

Louisville was a brighter place
with Joshua living there.
But then Henrietta grew ill,
so ill she could no longer work,
so ill that Jane returned
and Henrietta rode
the Ohio River again,
rode away from Joshua.
This time the river
carried Henrietta to Cincinnati
in Ohio—a free state!
She was used to sorrow,
used to the salt
of her own tears,
but not to kindness.
Jane paid
for Henrietta's treatment,
paid for the necessary medicine,
and Henrietta slowly healed.
And then the miracle came:
Jane signed her freedom papers.
Emancipation! Sweet liberty!

Ownership

Henrietta still worked for Jane,
but now as a free woman.
But was this liberty?
She was promised pay
but rarely got it.
After two years,
Henrietta set out
on her own.
And whenever she could,
she visited the river,
watching it flow
in tranquil freedom,
like her new life.
She worked for other people,
doing housekeeping,
earning wages,
buying little things
and a small chest
to tuck them in.
The chest held her greatest treasure,
her freedom papers:
proof that she owned herself,
a power that no one could take away.
Or so she thought.
Henrietta couldn't have known
about the plot
brewing against her.

Treachery

Jane's daughter, Josephine,
bristled because her mother
had freed Henrietta,
giving away property
Josephine considered her own—
property she could have sold for profit!
Josephine's father, William, had drafted
a legal document for his children,
stating that Henrietta
belonged to them.
But in Cincinnati,
Henrietta's freedom
could never be taken away.
As long as Henrietta lived on the
free side
of the Ohio River,
there could be no money
for Josephine.
But what if Henrietta
was back on the other side, in Kentucky,
where Josephine lived?
For five years,
Henrietta had enjoyed liberty.
For five years,
Josephine had plotted
to take that liberty away,
and now she saw how
to get quick cash for Henrietta.
Josephine lived just over the Ohio River,
in Kenton County, and she knew
the deputy sheriff, Zebulon Ward,
who purchased negroes
and resold them for a handsome profit,
not caring if they had freedom papers or not.
Ward agreed to pay Josephine $300

for ownership of Henrietta
without a guarantee
of ever possessing her.
Josephine pocketed the money
and wished Ward luck
claiming his property.

Ward *knew* he could capture Henrietta
and more than double his money.
He just had to invest a bit
in someone who could help.
One of Henrietta's employers,
Rebecca Boyd,
was happy to conspire,
and set a trap for Henrietta
in exchange for a fee.
It was Rebecca's job
to lure Henrietta into Kentucky.
Ward would be waiting,
Rebecca's payment in hand.

A Carriage Ride

Henrietta was thirty-three years old
in the spring of 1853,
had been to hell and back,
but she still trusted people,
still hoped for goodness and kindness—
even from employers like Rebecca Boyd
who had never paid her
with more than words
capped by the promise of "soon."
When, out of the blue,
Rebecca approached Henrietta
with a wide friendly smile,
inviting her to take
a leisurely carriage ride
on a Sunday afternoon,
Henrietta said, "Yes."
She took it as a welcome relief
from drudgery and lonely days.
Climbing inside the carriage,
Henrietta didn't question
why the curtains were drawn
and buttoned down
like a hearse.

PART THREE

STOLEN

River's Edge

Horse hooves clattered
over cobblestone streets,
kicking up dust
in the sloping light,
jostling the carriage,
drawing Henrietta toward the river
where a steamboat waited
at the sloped edge,
waited until the driver
directed the horses onboard.

Crossing

The steamboat delivered Henrietta
back over the river,
back to Kentucky,
back to the wrong side.
Henrietta saw no harm
in crossing the river
to Covington
just for the day—
Cincinnati residents
crossed the river
to shop in Covington
all the time.
She was one of them now,
a free Ohio citizen,
with papers at home
to prove it.
The steamboat landed
with the slightest bump,
and then the carriage disembarked.

Resale

On Kentucky soil,
the driver urged the horses
to carry Henrietta
straight past the town,
deep into the country,
deep where no one would see.
A pull on the reins,
a halt, and then
Henrietta heard voices
from the road.
Rebecca Boyd opened the carriage door
and stepped outside
to speak with three men
and laugh with them.
Through the open door,
Henrietta saw one of the three
hand a wad of cash to her.
Rebecca thanked him,
calling him Mr. Ward.
He ordered Henrietta out of the carriage,
with a devilish laugh
she would never forget,
along with his name.

Threats and Laughter

Henrietta stared at the three men,
studied the long, empty road,
so far from the river,
so far from where she lived free,
and knew that she had been abducted.
There was no way back to the freedom papers
in her small chest.
"Now, don't run,
or I'll shoot you," Ward said.
Henrietta replied,
"I've got nothing to run for,"
and again heard that devilish laugh.

A Dusty Road

Boyd climbed back
into the carriage.
that headed back
toward the river,
back toward freedom.
Henrietta watched the scattered dust
settle until the men ordered her
to start walking.

Sundown

The sun hung low
in the late afternoon sky.
Henrietta's head hung low
as she marched through Kentucky dirt
for many miles
into the town of Covington,
to a boardinghouse above a bar.
The men ordered Henrietta
up four flights of stairs,
into a room with a taunting
view of the river.
They snatched her bag,
wrenching it from her arm,
rifled through it,
dumped it on the bed,
searching for her papers.
She looked across the river,
back where she belonged,
where her freedom papers lay,
with all those little things
that belonged to her
stowed in that treasured chest.
The men would find her papers there
and would destroy them.
Darkness shrouded the river
that offered nothing more to Henrietta.

Another Prayer

Locked inside,
a guard outside,
Henrietta sank onto the bed
but felt no relief,
only unrelenting sorrow.
The landlady came
bearing crackers and tea,
but Henrietta did not touch them.
The woman left,
whispering low,
"What a shame."
All night
Henrietta lay awake
palms pressed tight,
praying to the good Lord,
Please, please . . ..
Would he deliver her
from this trouble?

PART FOUR

HOPE

Last Look

The sun reached for her
through a glass pane.
Henrietta dragged herself
out of bed,
faced the beaming light,
and took one last look
at old Cincinnati,
where she'd savored
the sweet taste of liberty.
The water ran high on the Ohio
she'd so foolishly crossed.
Steamboats readied to depart,
a boatload of cotton pulled in.
Carriages thronged the ferry dock,
waiting for passage.
A fiddler played
aboard a drifting lumber raft,
and someone danced.
She took these bittersweet sights in,
letting the memories run deep.
No one could wrench them from her.
Then a harsh knock
at the door
knocked her gaze
off the river,
back inside.

Trust

On the second day
of her imprisonment,
they took her to Florence, Kentucky,
to an inn where they locked her in a room.
There was no river view to soothe her,
no flowing path to lead her home.
Where was hope now?
She tensed
when the door creaked open,
and the young innkeeper
stepped in with eyes
that promised hope.
He told her he suspected
something treacherous
had happened to her
and asked how she had come
to be there.
At first, Henrietta
was too scared to speak.
She knew her abductors
would whip her mercilessly
if she told where she came from,
if she said she had been free.
But the innkeeper promised
he would help her,
not betray her,
and though false promises
had brought her here,
this was a chance to be heard.
So she dared to tell him
her story.

Promise

On the rocky ride,
farther south,
toward Lexington, Kentucky,
where the slave markets were,
Henrietta carried hope,
fragile as an egg.
Her heart held a promise from Williams,
the innkeeper who'd vowed
to find proof of her freedom.
He'd asked for names of people
she knew in Cincinnati,
and he was headed there
to speak with them.
If they verified that she was free,
he would come find her
at a Lexington market
and tell the authorities
that she had been kidnapped.
An eggshell-thin hope
was better than none
on this dusty
desolate path,
farther and farther
away from the river,
away from freedom,
with only one meager creek
along the way,
coursing slow, like tears.
Would Williams really help her?
Would he ever come?

Slave Pen

Seventy shaking miles
and one sunset later,
Henrietta's transport ended
in Lexington, Kentucky.
She stepped out of the carriage,
past a looming fence
into a large building where
a crowd of colored persons
stood in the dim light.
An iron gate clanged shut
behind her,
and her heart sank.
She'd heard of this place,
this pen,
owned by the biggest,
busiest slave trader
in Kentucky, Lewis Robards.
Would she be sold
before Williams came?

Confinement

Sunrise brought relief.
Robards took Henrietta
from the pen
into his house,
where she was watched
by a colored woman
whose name was Beck—
both of them at his beck
and call.
Henrietta sewed clothes
to be worn by people of all ages,
dressed up
for inspection
and sale.
Weeks went by
Without any sign of Williams,
without a glimmer of hope.
Had he journeyed to the pen
and, not seeing her, gone away?

A Fleeting Smile

Henrietta still hoped,
but that hope shrank
back into a tiny corner
of her mind.
Then one morning
as she took her breakfast,
she saw Williams
in the yard
looking through the window.
Hope looking right at her!
He turned away quickly,
but she could not erase the joy
flashing on her face,
could not stop Beck from spotting it.
Beck told Robards:
"Henrietta smiled at a stranger."
She had given herself and Williams away.
Infuriated, Robards forced Henrietta into his buggy,
bonneted to hide her face.
Thirty miles away from the pen,
thirty miles from Williams,
from hope,
the buggy passed through the countryside.
Birds chattered in the trees,
squirrels ran through the woods,
and horses galloped in a field,
flaunting their freedom.

PART FIVE

HOPELESS

Terror

Robards took Henrietta
to the small town of Harrodsburg, Kentucky
and hid her there.
But one dark night
he reappeared,
steaming angry,
and ordered her into his carriage.
They bolted through the woods,
Robards spitting words at her:
Williams had approached the authorities,
told them Henrietta was abducted,
that she had been free.
A judge had ordered:
Henrietta *must* appear in court
for a hearing to determine the truth.
Robards cursed her
and the problems she caused him.
Henrietta braced herself to be killed.

A Warning

Henrietta was alive when
Robards deposited her
back in his Lexington pen.
Alive but chilled by his warning:
she had better watch
what came out of her mouth in court.
Those spiked words
lodged in Henrietta's gut.
She'd heard of Negroes
who spoke freely
to judges.
She knew their fate:
their owners made sure
they never spoke again.

News

Henrietta paced,
up and down the pen,
day after day after day.
And one extraordinary day,
her mother came in!
If only Henrietta could speak freely,
but she dared not share
the news that she had ever been free.
Robards's threats had scared her into silence.
What if a guard heard her?
But her mother was not afraid
to speak the truth,
the heartbreaking news—
Henrietta's father was dead.

Waiting

Henrietta kept silent as a stick
during the courtroom hearing.
Williams's insistence
that Henrietta had been abducted
into Kentucky slavery
was strong enough
to warrant the trial of *Wood v. Robards*
without her words.

Henrietta awaited her day in court
locked in a jail cell.
Her lawyers told her:
Robards demanded that Zebulon Ward
take responsibility
and become the defendant in her case.
If she had been kidnapped,
Ward had done the deed.
Henrietta shuddered at that name.
How could she win her freedom
against the devil himself?
The law moved slowly.
For a year,
Henrietta sat behind bars,
saw no sun,
and heard Ward's demonic laugh in her head.

Voiceless

The case of *Wood v. Ward*
began on June 24, 1854.
Ward glared hate
from the defense table.
New Orleans was hell,
but *this* was a deeper hell,
for here sat its king
vying to possess her.
But she still could not state her story.
Negroes were brought to the courthouse cellar
and flogged to death
for speaking up in court.
Better to belong to the devil
than be buried in a ditch.

The judge said she did not make her case.
Since she did not testify
that she had had been kidnapped,
there was no proof.
And there was no federal law
forcing Kentucky to grant her freedom
because she had lived in a free state.
He ruled that she rightfully belonged to Ward.

The case was appealed to a higher court.
She waited and waited,
six more sunless months behind bars,
until she was brought back to court,
only to repeat the fruitless,
muted process.
On January 20, 1855,
came the verdict:
a ruling against Henrietta.
She would not be freed.
Ward grinned in victory.
Henrietta refused to show fear

but vowed to defeat him.
Someday, somehow,
she would wipe that smile off Satan's face.

A Strong Woman

Ward took Henrietta home to
Frankfort, Kentucky,
where he flaunted his control over her.
He forced her to obey his wife
and care for his young children.
Henrietta lost all hope
of ever going home to Cincinnati.
She talked back to Ward's wife,
arguing until the woman
threatened to whip her.
Henrietta raised her tall, two-hundred-pound frame up
and said, "It takes men to whip me."

Henrietta, too difficult to keep,
was sold again in the fall of 1855.
Sent far from Kentucky
in case she started trouble again,
mouthing about freedom papers and kidnapping.
The devil shipped her down the Mississippi River,
where no one cared how Negroes got there.
In Mississippi, they just set them to work.

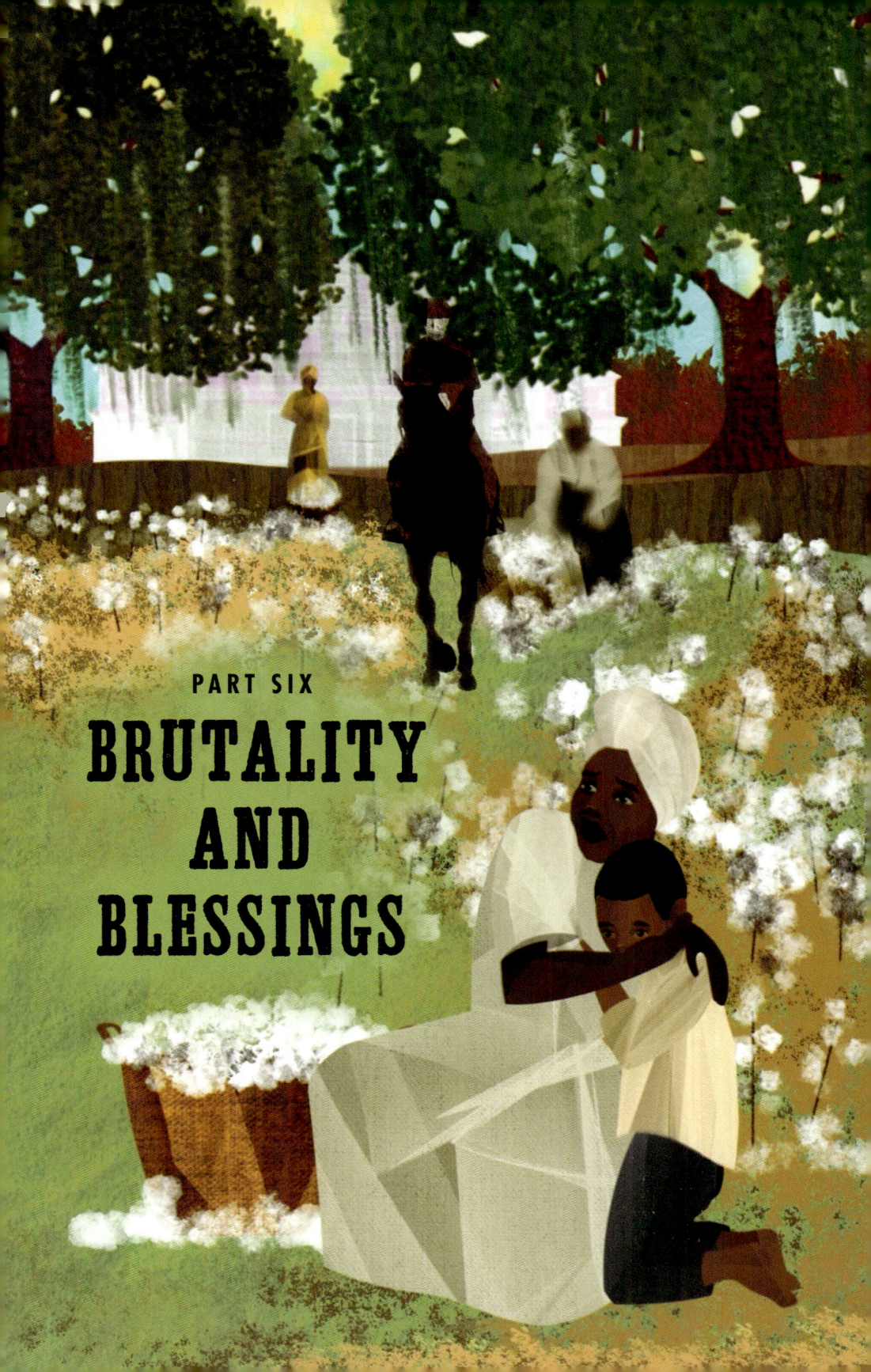

PART SIX

BRUTALITY AND BLESSINGS

Fresh Wounds

Sold to Gerard Brandon,
owner of a huge cotton plantation
in Natchez, Mississippi,
with eight hundred enslaved Negroes,
Henrietta faced fieldwork now,
hoeing weeds
and clearing soil for new crops
under the burning sun.
She had never worked so hard!
She tried to do a good job,
but nothing would satisfy
her overseer's demands.
Nothing seemed to stop
his whip on her bare flesh,
every stroke leaving a gash
like a knife across her back.
And then, to increase the torture,
he sprinkled salt
on her wounds.
So many times
she got flogged
until she thought she would die.

Family

Henrietta gave birth
to a son named Arthur
on January 8, 1856.
Who was Arthur's father?
Henrietta never said.
She was moved to the house,
rescued from the fields,
an unexpected gift,
a blessing, like Arthur.
Thank you, dear Lord.
At last, she had someone of her own,
a family to treasure again.

Long Walk to Texas

Years went by.
Henrietta didn't know about the war being waged
between the Southern and Northern states.
She was unaware the South had left the Union
and called itself the Confederacy.
Word about the January 1863 proclamation
that freed all the slaves in the Southern states
did not make it to Natchez.
Not until July 1863 did news about the war reach her.
She heard Brandon's panicked conversations:
The Union army of the North was taking over Mississippi!
Brandon had to leave—now!
Many plantation owners
were fleeing to Texas,
figuring that it was so far away
the Union army would never make it there.
Brandon decided to go there, too.
He picked three hundred enslaved workers
to walk nearly four hundred miles,
to Robertson County, Texas.
Henrietta was among them.
But Brandon didn't want children
slowing them down.
Henrietta begged Brandon
to let Arthur come.
Her pleas were relentless,
heartbroken, strong.
Brandon finally agreed.
Clutching her son,
Henrietta set forth.
She didn't care how far,
she would walk forever
as long as she had Arthur.

A Poor Freedom

The Union army burst into Texas on June 19, 1865,
galloping through cities and towns,
giving the news to all enslaved people:
Abraham Lincoln, the President of the United States,
had issued a proclamation two and a half years ago
ending slavery in all Southern states.
Free? Henrietta struggled to absorb the word.
She rejoiced—for a moment.
Then she questioned:
free to live how and where with her son?
She had no money,
no means to leave,
no means to live.
Certainly, she had no way home to Cincinnati.
Brandon made her an offer:
if she would go to Natchez with him and
work three years for pay on his plantation,
she and Arthur would have a home
and money saved to travel up the rivers.

Return

Over the next three years,
Brandon never paid Henrietta a penny
for all the hard work she did.
This latest injustice
churned through her insides,
but she needed a place to live with Arthur
so she kept quiet.
Setting her mind on a way out,
she raised her own hogs and chickens,
sold them in the market,
and saved twenty-five dollars.
It was enough to take her and Arthur
up the Mississippi River
to meet the Ohio River,
bringing her closer and closer to home.
Along the way, she thought about
that devil, Zebulon Ward,
who had sent her to
ten years of torture
so he could profit and keep her silent.
Each watery mile stirred her to an awakening:
Ward should pay.

PART SEVEN

JUSTICE

Henrietta's Turn

Back in Cincinnati,
back beside her river,
there was no right or wrong side anymore.
It had taken Henrietta sixteen years
to taste liberty again
in the city where she'd first been liberated,
but Henrietta's awakening had grown into determination:
Zebulon Ward *must* pay.
She thought back to all that time locked in jail,
waiting for a day in court where she was bound to lose
because she could not speak.
She remembered his demonic grin.
It was time for a second day in court,
time to tell her story.
Henrietta wanted reparations,
repayment for lost wages
and for her suffering.
Most of all,
she wanted acknowledgment
of the crimes committed against her.

Delays

Once a lawyer agreed to take her case,
a summons was issued on June 3, 1870,
for Ward to answer her lawsuit.
For eight years, his lawyers
delayed the case, fighting to dismiss it
in every possible way.
Eight years went by until time
ran out for Ward, but not for Henrietta.

Hearing

On April 15, 1878, a jury
of twelve white men
was chosen to hear
fifty-eight-year-old Henrietta's case.
By the end of the next day,
this jury had heard all the evidence.
By the day after that, closing statements,
followed by deliberation:
Could a formerly enslaved person
be entitled to restitution?
If one, then why not all?

Restitution

Twelve jurors felt the weight of precedent
once the gates of justice opened
to the rivers of restitution,
but they also felt Henrietta's suffering,
felt the immeasurable weight of injustice.

They returned a quick verdict,
scrawled on a paper in the foreman's hand,
a verdict in favor of Henrietta!
The jurors could not restore all she had lost—
the stolen years and family,
the blood and tears she'd shed.
Money could not heal her scars.
But Henrietta had won over the jury
with her voice and with her story.
She'd won a measure of restitution,
won a judgment entered into public record,
permanent evidence, just like her freedom papers.

With a slam of the gavel, a portion
of the justice she deserved was finally served.
Henrietta Wood had made her case
against Zebulon Ward.

At last, the sweet taste of victory.

Afterword

Henrietta Wood sued Zebulon Ward for $20,000. The jury awarded her $2,500, a fraction of what she asked for and deserved. Although this sliver of justice, recorded for posterity, does not begin to make up for the injustices Henrietta suffered, to date it is the largest financial award granted by an American court as reparations for enslavement. It was enough money to send her son, Arthur H. Simms, to law school.

Henrietta moved to Chicago with Arthur. He attended Union College of Law, the shared law school of the University of Chicago and Northwestern University, graduating in the class of 1889. Arthur became a successful and well-respected attorney and eventually married. Henrietta was thrilled that her two grandchildren, Arthur Jr. and Neata, were born into freedom. She even witnessed Neata's marriage before passing away that same year, 1912.

Her son, Arthur, thrived in Chicago for forty more years. When he died in 1951 at the age of ninety-five, he was the nation's oldest practicing Negro lawyer.

Henrietta's descendants did her proud. One became a Tuskegee Airman during World War II, another was a well-known Chicago jazz musician. Many more were professionals, including a librarian, a doctor, and a computer expert.

Henrietta Wood's remarkable story of survival, and ultimate victory, is a testament to the strength of the human spirit, as well as a defining moment in American history which must never be forgotten.

Missing Pieces

I gleaned most of Henrietta's story from the interviews she granted two Cincinnati reporters, one in 1876 and the other in 1879. However, there are details which Henrietta did not know. One of them was her exact age. Moses Tousey's estate listed her as age fourteen when he died in 1834 which is why I used 1820 as her birth year.

Henrietta also did not know that her disappearance in the spring of 1853 sent Cincinnati's free Black community into an uproar, leading to an investigation by local authorities. Rebecca Boyd, John Gilbert, the carriage driver, and Frank Rust, a coconspirator, were arrested for Henrietta's abduction under an 1831 Ohio state law against kidnapping free people of color.

Unfortunately, Jacob Flynn, the judge for their trial, was proslavery, so much so that he physically attacked John Joliffe, one of the prosecutors, when he saw Joliffe out shopping, calling him a "damn abolitionist."

Joliffe recovered but left the prosecution team. Fined for the assault, Flynn remained on the case. He ruled that that this law had been voided by an 1842 Supreme Court decision in *Prigg v. Pennsylvania*, which allowed Blacks to be taken from a free state and into enslavement. Boyd, Gilbert, and Rust were found not guilty by the jury.

Juneteenth

Juneteenth National Independence Day is a holiday celebrating the end of enslavement in America. It commemorates June 19, 1865, the day Union troops arrived in Texas to enforce Abraham Lincoln's Emancipation Proclamation, ending enslavement in all the Southern states.

Texas had been the Confederate state farthest from the North, and enslavers like Gerard Brandon thought they would be able to keep their enslaved workers uninformed about their freedom. But this deception ended with the arrival of Union General Gordon Granger and his troops in Galveston, Texas. Two and a half years after the proclamation was issued on January 1, 1863—and over two months after the Civil War ended on April 9, 1865—250,000 formerly enslaved people, including Henrietta Wood, learned they were free.

Also known as Emancipation Day, Freedom Day, Black Independence Day, and Jubilee Day, Juneteenth has been commemorated on June 19 each year since 1865. President Joseph R. Biden signed the Juneteenth National Independence Day Act into law on June 17, 2021, declaring Juneteenth a federal holiday—America's first since 1983 when Martin Luther King Jr. Day was established.

Bibliography

All quotations used in the book can be found in the following sources marked with an asterisk (*).

Interviews with Henrietta Wood

*Hearn, Lafcadio. "Story of a Slave." *Cincinnati Commercial* [Ohio], April 2, 1876, p. 2.

*"Kidnapped and Sold into Slavery, part 2." *Ripley Bee* [Ohio], February 27, 1879.

*"Kidnapped and Sold into Slavery, part 3." *Ripley Bee* [Ohio], March 6, 1879.

*"Kidnapped and Sold into Slavery, part 4." *Ripley Bee* [Ohio], March 20, 1879.

Court Cases

Wood v. Ward
There is a notation documenting Wood's first lawsuit in the Fayette County (Kentucky) Circuit Court Order Book, vol. 37 (March 4, 1853–March 3, 1855). No case files remain, but Henrietta discusses it in her interviews, and it is referred to in the records of the second lawsuit.

Wood's second lawsuit is recorded in Case File 1431, US Circuit Court, Southern District of Ohio, Cincinnati. She discusses it in her interviews.

Books

Beckert, Sven, and Seth Rockman, eds. *Slavery's Capitalism: A New History of American Economic Development.* Philadelphia: University of Pennsylvania Press, 2016.

Grear, Charles D., ed. *The Fate of Texas: The Civil War and the Lone Star State.* Fayetteville: University of Arkansas Press, 2008.

James, D. Clayton. *Antebellum Natchez.* Baton Rouge: Louisiana State University Press, 1993.

Johnson, Walter. *River of Dark Dreams: Slavery and Empire in the Cotton Kingdom.* Cambridge, MA: Belknap Press of Harvard University Press, 2013.

McDaniel, W. Caleb. *Sweet Taste of Liberty: A True Story of Slavery and Restitution in America.* New York: Oxford University Press, 2019.

Pargas, Damian Alan. *Slavery and Forced Migration in the Antebellum South.* New York: Cambridge University Press, 2015.

Salafia, Matthew. *Slavery's Borderland: Freedom and Bondage Along the Ohio River.* Philadelphia: University of Pennsylvania Press, 2013.

Wayne, Michael. *The Reshaping of Plantation Society: The Natchez District, 1860–1880.* Baton Rouge: Louisiana State University Press, 1983

Articles

Barton, Keith C. "Good Cooks and Washers: Slave Hiring, Domestic Labor, and the Market in Bourbon County, Kentucky." *Journal of American History* 84, no. 2: 436–460.

Cole, Stephanie. "Servants and Slaves in Louisville: Race, Ethnicity, and Household Labor in an Antebellum Border City." *Ohio Valley History* 11, no. 1: 3–25.

Newspapers and Journals (1800s)

*Cincinnati Commercial

*Cincinnati Daily Enquirer

*Cincinnati Daily Gazette

Covington Journal [Kentucky]

Indianapolis News

Kentucky Statesman

Louisville Courier-Journal

Louisville Morning Courier

Natchez Daily Courier [Mississippi]

Mississippi Free Trader and Natchez Gazette

New Orleans Daily Picayune

New-Orleans Commercial Bulletin

New York Times

*Pittsburgh Legal Journal

*Ripley Bee [Ohio]

Acknowledgments

Thank you to W. Caleb McDaniel, associate professor of history at Rice University and author of the Pulitzer Prize-winning nonfiction book *Sweet Taste of Liberty: A True Story of Slavery and Restitution in America*, for sharing his open notebook detailing the research for his book on Henrietta Wood: wiki.wcaleb.rice.edu.

Thank you to the Bank Street Writers Lab at Bank Street College of Education for providing me with their thoughts and feedback on this book.

Illustrator's Note

As a Black woman, it was an honor to illustrate such an important story that needed to be told. My travels through the world have paved the way for a deeper understanding of the intricate tapestry of history, culture, and resistance.

Illustrating Henrietta's life, I got to bear witness to her resilience and indomitable spirit.

Each stroke of my pen carries the weight of her story, intertwining sorrow and hope, as we confront the harsh realities of our past while envisioning a future of justice and healing.

Through my art, I aim to illuminate the often-overlooked narratives of Black women in history, celebrating their strength and tenacity. This book is not just a tribute to Henrietta Wood, but a call to acknowledge the ongoing struggle for equity and recognition. It is my hope that this story will inspire a dialogue about reparations and the significance of reclaiming our stories for generations to come.

Selene Castrovilla is the author of *Seeking Freedom: The Untold Story of Fortress Monroe and the Ending of Slavery in America*, an ALSC Notable Children's Book, a Virginia Readers' Choice, a CCBC Choice, a New York Public Library Best Book for Kids, and a Bank Street Best Book of the Year. She has written several other books for Calkins Creek, including *Revolutionary Friends: General George Washington and the Marquis de Lafayette* and *George Washington's Spectacular Spectacles: The Glasses That Saved America*. A mother of two sons, Selene lives on a Long Island lagoon with swans, egrets, and a humongous hound named Bean. Learn more at selenecastrovilla.com.

Erin K. Robinson trained at the Parsons School of Design and the Corcoran School of the Arts & Design. Her illustrations have been featured in the *New York Times* and the *Washington Post* and in many books, including *A Library* written by Nikki Giovanni and *This Hair Belongs* written by JaNay Brown-Wood. She has also been nominated for an Emmy in the news and documentary category, and she designed the 2022 Kwanzaa stamp for the United States Postal Service. Visit brooklyndolly.com.

For information about permission to reproduce selections from this book,
please contact permissions@astrapublishinghouse.com.

Calkins Creek
An imprint of Astra Books for Young Readers,
a division of Astra Publishing House
astrapublishinghouse.com
Printed in Malaysia

ISBN: 978-1-6626-8074-8 (hc)
ISBN: 978-1-6626-8073-1 (eBook)
Library of Congress Control Number: 2025935739

First edition

10 9 8 7 6 5 4 3 2 1

Design by Barbara Grzeslo and Michelle Mayhall
The text is set in Futura Std.
The titles are set in Archive Antiqua Extra Cond.
The illustrations are created digitally in Procreate.